Conversation my robot friend

Exploring the Impact of ChatGPT on Our Lives and Futures

Contents

Introduction

ChatGPT is a cutting-edge technology that is changing the way we interact with artificial intelligence. Developed by OpenAI, it is a language model that uses advanced machine learning algorithms to generate human-like text. With the ability to understand and respond to natural language inputs, ChatGPT is revolutionizing the field of AI and paving the way for a new era of human-robot interaction.

To understand ChatGPT, it is important to know what a language model is and how it works. A language model is a type of artificial intelligence that is trained to generate or predict text based on patterns it has learned from vast amounts of data. This data can be anything from books, articles, and websites to conversations, social media posts, and more. With this training, language models are able to generate coherent and natural-sounding text that can be used for a variety of purposes.

ChatGPT takes this concept a step further by using a transformer-based architecture, which allows it to process text in a more human-like way. This architecture allows ChatGPT to understand the context of a conversation, which is crucial for generating meaningful and relevant responses. With its advanced training and advanced architecture, ChatGPT is able to generate human-like text with a high degree of accuracy and fluency, making it a powerful tool for many different applications.

One of the most exciting things about ChatGPT is its potential to change the way we interact with artificial intelligence. With its ability to understand and respond to natural language inputs, ChatGPT is making it possible for us to have conversations with robots in a way that feels more natural and intuitive. This has the potential to revolutionize the field of AI and open up new possibilities for how we use technology in our daily lives.

Another key aspect of ChatGPT is its ability to learn and adapt over time. With its advanced machine learning algorithms, ChatGPT is able to learn from its interactions and improve its responses over time. This means that as more people use ChatGPT and it processes more data, it will become even more accurate and sophisticated in its responses. This is an important factor that sets ChatGPT apart from other language models and makes it a truly cutting-edge technology.

ChatGPT also has the potential to be used in a variety of applications, from customer service and support to entertainment and education. For example, ChatGPT can be used to provide 24/7 customer service, respond to questions and provide information, or even generate creative content such as poems or stories. The possibilities for ChatGPT are endless, and it is likely that we will see many new and innovative uses for this technology in the years to come.

ChatGPT is also highly customizable, making it a versatile tool for a wide range of applications. For instance, it can be fine-tuned to specific domains and tasks, such as finance, legal, or medical. This allows organizations to train ChatGPT on specific data sets and use it for specialized purposes, such as generating financial reports or analyzing legal cases. With its ability to handle large amounts of data and provide quick and accurate results, ChatGPT is an ideal solution for businesses looking to streamline their processes and increase efficiency.

Another area where ChatGPT is making a big impact is in the field of virtual assistants. With its advanced language processing capabilities, ChatGPT can be integrated into virtual assistants to provide more natural and intuitive interactions. This allows users to interact with their virtual assistants in a way that feels more like speaking with a human, which can greatly improve the overall user experience.

In the area of education, ChatGPT has the potential to revolutionize the way students learn and interact with information. By providing quick and accurate responses to students' questions, ChatGPT can help students find the information they need more quickly and easily. This can also help to reduce the workload of teachers and provide students with a more personalized learning experience.

Lastly, ChatGPT has the potential to be a valuable tool in the fight against climate change and environmental degradation. By processing large amounts of data and providing quick and accurate results, ChatGPT can be used to analyze environmental data, such as air and water quality, and provide valuable insights into the state of our planet. This information can then be used to develop new strategies for reducing our impact on the environment and protecting our planet for future generations.

The reliability and accuracy of ChatGPT

ChatGPT is a powerful language model developed by OpenAI that has taken the world by storm with its remarkable ability to generate human-like responses. The model was trained on a vast corpus of text data, allowing it to respond to various questions with natural language responses. However, with its increasing popularity, it is essential to examine its reliability and accuracy.

Reliability is defined as the consistency of a model's performance. In the case of ChatGPT, it refers to the consistency of its responses to similar inputs. The model is designed to generate coherent and contextually relevant responses, but there is a possibility that its responses might not be accurate or appropriate. In some cases, ChatGPT may generate responses that are offensive, irrelevant, or factually incorrect. Hence, it is important to consider the reliability of the model when deploying it in real-world applications.

One way to improve the reliability of ChatGPT is through fine-tuning. Fine-tuning involves retraining the model on a smaller corpus of data that is specific to a particular task. This allows the model to become more specialized, and therefore more reliable, in that task. For example, fine-tuning ChatGPT on medical data could lead to a model that is better equipped to respond to medical-related queries.

Accuracy is defined as the measure of a model's ability to generate responses that are true to the input data. In the case of ChatGPT, accuracy refers to the degree to which its responses are factually correct. Although the model has been trained on a massive corpus of text data, there is always a possibility that it may generate incorrect responses. For example, the model may not have seen a specific query in its training data and may generate a response that is factually incorrect.

One way to improve the accuracy of ChatGPT is through data augmentation. Data augmentation involves adding more diverse data to the model's training corpus, allowing it to learn from a wider range of examples. This can help the model to generate more accurate responses to a broader range of queries.

Another way to improve the accuracy of ChatGPT is through the use of external knowledge sources. The model can be designed to use external knowledge sources, such as databases or APIs, to generate more accurate responses. For example, ChatGPT could be integrated with a database of medical knowledge, allowing it to generate more accurate responses to medical-related queries.

ChatGPT's ability to learn and adapt

Artificial intelligence has come a long way since its inception. With advancements in technology, AI systems have become more advanced, sophisticated, and able to perform a wider range of tasks. One such AI system is ChatGPT, a language model created by OpenAI. One of the unique features of ChatGPT is its ability to learn and adapt. In this chapter, we will explore this ability in depth and understand how it sets ChatGPT apart from other AI systems.

The process of machine learning involves teaching AI systems to perform specific tasks by providing them with vast amounts of data. The AI system uses this data to create mathematical models that can identify patterns and make predictions. The more data an AI system has access to, the more accurate its predictions will be. This process is what makes ChatGPT so powerful and versatile.

ChatGPT is trained on an immense amount of data, which includes text from books, websites, news articles, and more. This training allows ChatGPT to understand the nuances of human language and respond in a way that is both natural and intelligent. Unlike other AI systems that are limited to specific tasks, ChatGPT can respond to a wide range of questions and perform a variety of tasks, such as translation, summarization, and even creative writing.

In addition to its vast data set, ChatGPT is designed to be flexible and adaptable. The AI system can continually learn from its interactions with users, allowing it to improve its performance over time. This means that ChatGPT can provide more accurate and relevant responses as it becomes more familiar with a user's preferences and habits.

One example of ChatGPT's adaptability can be seen in its ability to generate personalized responses. By analyzing a user's behavior and preferences, ChatGPT can tailor its responses to suit the individual's needs. This can be especially useful in customer service situations where the AI system can provide quick and accurate responses to common questions.

Another example of ChatGPT's ability to learn and adapt is its ability to recognize and respond to different writing styles and tones. Whether a user is writing in a formal or informal manner, ChatGPT can adapt its responses to match the tone and style of the writing. This allows ChatGPT to engage in conversations that are both natural and engaging.

One of the most remarkable aspects of ChatGPT is its ability to continually learn and improve. This is achieved through the use of machine learning algorithms that allow it to process vast amounts of data and identify patterns and relationships within that data. These algorithms then allow ChatGPT to adjust its behavior and responses to better match the context and requirements of each situation.

This process of learning and adapting is ongoing, with ChatGPT continuously updating its understanding of the world and its own abilities. This means that, over time, it becomes more and more capable of accurately predicting and responding to a wide range of scenarios.

Another important aspect of ChatGPT's ability to learn and adapt is its capacity for self-correction. By constantly evaluating its own performance and identifying areas for improvement, it is able to fine-tune its responses and improve its accuracy. This is particularly valuable in complex, rapidly-changing environments where accurate information and quick responses are critical.

In addition to its ability to learn and adapt, ChatGPT also has the potential to collaborate with other AI systems and technologies. By working together, these systems can share data and knowledge, further improving their accuracy and capabilities. This is particularly relevant in industries where multiple AI systems are used to manage complex processes, as it enables each system to learn from the others and collaborate in real-time to deliver better outcomes.

The impact of ChatGPT on the global economy

Artificial intelligence has been making waves in various industries and sectors, transforming the way people live, work and communicate. One such development that has taken the world by storm is the creation of ChatGPT. A language model developed by OpenAI, ChatGPT has revolutionized the way humans interact with machines and has the potential to have a significant impact on the global economy.

To understand the impact of ChatGPT on the global economy, it is important to first understand what ChatGPT is and how it works. ChatGPT is a large language model that has been trained on vast amounts of data to generate human-like responses to questions and tasks. It uses machine learning algorithms and natural language processing techniques to understand the context and meaning behind words, allowing it to respond in a more natural and human-like manner.

The primary impact of ChatGPT on the global economy is in the area of automation. As ChatGPT becomes more sophisticated and can perform more complex tasks, it has the potential to automate many jobs that are currently performed by humans. This could have a major impact on the global labor market, with some jobs becoming obsolete as they are taken over by AI. However, it is also likely to lead to the creation of new jobs in fields such as AI development and maintenance.

Another important impact of ChatGPT on the global economy is in the area of customer service. With its ability to understand and respond to customer queries in a natural and human-like manner, ChatGPT has the potential to transform the way businesses interact with their customers. By automating many customer service tasks, businesses can save time and money, while also improving the customer experience. This could lead to increased customer satisfaction and loyalty, as well as higher sales and profits for businesses.

The impact of ChatGPT on the global economy is also likely to be felt in the areas of research and development. As ChatGPT becomes more advanced and is able to perform more complex tasks, it has the potential to assist scientists and researchers in areas such as data analysis and hypothesis testing. This could lead to faster and more accurate research, resulting in new breakthroughs and innovations in a range of fields.

The impact of ChatGPT on the global economy is a topic that is gaining increasing attention as the capabilities and applications of this powerful AI model continue to expand. At its core, ChatGPT is a machine learning tool that can generate human-like text, based on large amounts of input data and the patterns that it has learned from that data. This makes it an incredibly versatile tool that can be applied in a wide range of industries and sectors, from customer service and marketing to finance and healthcare.

One of the key ways in which ChatGPT is expected to impact the global economy is through its ability to automate many of the repetitive and time-consuming tasks that are currently performed by human workers. By streamlining these processes and making them more efficient, ChatGPT has the potential to significantly reduce costs for businesses and organizations, while freeing up human workers to focus on more complex and creative tasks. This, in turn, could lead to an increase in productivity, efficiency, and overall economic growth.

In addition to its potential to automate tasks, ChatGPT is also likely to have a major impact on the way that businesses interact with their customers. By providing a virtual assistant that can respond to customer inquiries and resolve issues in real-time, ChatGPT has the potential to revolutionize customer service, making it faster, more efficient, and more personalized. This could help businesses to build stronger relationships with their customers, increase customer loyalty, and ultimately drive sales and revenue.

Another area where ChatGPT is likely to have a major impact is in the field of data analysis. With its ability to process and analyze vast amounts of data in real-time, ChatGPT has the potential to provide businesses with new insights into their operations, customer behavior, and market trends. This, in turn, could help businesses to make more informed decisions, optimize their operations, and stay ahead of their competitors.

Finally, ChatGPT's ability to learn and adapt is also likely to have a major impact on the global economy. By continuously learning from new data and adjusting its algorithms accordingly, ChatGPT has the potential to become an ever more powerful tool, providing businesses and organizations with new insights and capabilities.

The role of ChatGPT in marketing and advertising

The development of artificial intelligence technology, particularly language-based models like ChatGPT, has been a game-changer in various industries, and marketing and advertising are no exception. As the technology continues to evolve, it has the potential to significantly impact how brands reach and engage with their customers. In this chapter, we will delve into the role of ChatGPT in marketing and advertising, exploring its current and future applications and the benefits and limitations of this technology.

ChatGPT in Customer Engagement

One of the key areas where ChatGPT is already making an impact is in customer engagement. By leveraging its natural language processing capabilities, ChatGPT can be integrated into chatbots that can interact with customers in a conversational manner. This opens up new avenues for brands to reach their customers and provide them with personalized experiences. For instance, a customer can initiate a conversation with a brand's chatbot through various channels like messaging apps, websites, and mobile apps. The chatbot can then use ChatGPT to understand the customer's query and provide relevant responses in real-time. This not only improves the overall customer experience but also helps brands to gather valuable customer insights that can inform their marketing and advertising strategies.

ChatGPT in Content Creation

Another area where ChatGPT is making a big impact is in content creation. With its ability to generate text based on specific inputs, ChatGPT can be used to create compelling and relevant content for marketing and advertising purposes. For instance, brands can use ChatGPT to generate product descriptions, ad copy, and even entire articles. This can significantly streamline the content creation process and help brands to produce high-quality content at a faster pace. Additionally, ChatGPT can be trained on a brand's language and tone, making it possible to generate content that is in line with the brand's voice and messaging.

The Benefits and Limitations of ChatGPT in Marketing and Advertising

While the applications of ChatGPT in marketing and advertising are vast and promising, there are also limitations to consider. One of the biggest benefits of ChatGPT is its ability to automate and scale many of the manual and time-consuming tasks associated with content creation and customer engagement. This can significantly improve the efficiency of marketing and advertising operations, freeing up resources for other important tasks.

However, there are also limitations to consider, particularly when it comes to the accuracy and reliability of the technology. While ChatGPT has been trained on large amounts of data and can generate content that is highly relevant, it is still limited by the quality and diversity of the data it was trained on. As a result, there may be instances where ChatGPT generates content that is inaccurate or insensitive, which could damage a brand's reputation. Additionally, the technology is still in its early stages, and there is a lack of standards and regulations around its use in marketing and advertising. This could lead to concerns around data privacy, the influence of AI on human decision-making, and the potential for AI to perpetuate biases and stereotypes.

The Future of ChatGPT in Marketing and Advertising

Despite its limitations, the future of ChatGPT in marketing and advertising is bright. As the technology continues to evolve, it will likely become even more sophisticated, making it possible to deliver even more personalized and relevant customer experiences. Additionally, as regulations and standards are established around the use of AI in marketing and advertising, brands can feel more confident about using the technology to engage with their customers. Ultimately, the role of ChatGPT in marketing and advertising will continue to evolve, and it will be fascinating to see how this technology continues to shape the industry in the coming years.

The advancement of technology has brought with it numerous changes to the world of marketing and advertising. With the emergence of powerful artificial intelligence models like ChatGPT, the possibilities are becoming even more diverse and exciting. ChatGPT has the ability to analyze large amounts of data and generate personalized advertisements and marketing strategies, creating a unique and effective approach to reaching target audiences.

One of the most significant advantages of using ChatGPT in marketing is its ability to understand human language and emotions. This allows it to generate messages that resonate with individuals on a deeper level, improving the chances of success. Furthermore, ChatGPT can analyze the results of each marketing campaign in real-time, allowing for quick adjustments to be made if necessary.

Another important factor in marketing is the ability to personalize advertisements. ChatGPT can analyze an individual's browsing history and social media activity to determine their interests and preferences. This information can be used to generate personalized advertisements that cater to each individual's needs and interests, making the advertising experience much more relevant and enjoyable.

In addition to personalized advertisements, ChatGPT can also be used to analyze market trends and predict future purchasing behavior. This information can be used to generate strategic marketing plans that take advantage of upcoming trends and target audiences effectively. This can be especially beneficial for businesses that are looking to stay ahead of their competition and gain a competitive edge.

However, it's important to note that while ChatGPT offers numerous benefits in marketing and advertising, it is not a perfect solution. There are still some limitations to its use, such as the need for high-quality training data, and the potential for biases to be introduced into the AI model if the training data is not diverse enough. Additionally, the cost of using ChatGPT for marketing and advertising can be a barrier for small businesses, which may not have the resources to invest in such a technology.

The future of language processing with ChatGPT

As technology continues to advance, we are seeing significant advancements in the field of natural language processing. One of the most promising developments in this area is the creation of large language models like ChatGPT. These models have the ability to understand and generate human language with remarkable accuracy, making them incredibly useful for a wide range of applications. In this chapter, we will explore the future of language processing with ChatGPT and how it is set to change the way we interact with technology and with each other.

One of the most exciting possibilities of ChatGPT is its ability to process large amounts of data and generate coherent, meaningful responses in real-time. This opens up a world of opportunities for businesses and individuals alike, enabling them to automate tasks, save time and improve efficiency. For example, ChatGPT can be used to generate reports, summaries and even entire articles, freeing up human employees to focus on more creative and complex tasks.

Another key area in which ChatGPT is expected to have a major impact is customer service. Chatbots powered by large language models like ChatGPT can provide quick and accurate answers to customer queries, freeing up human agents to handle more complex issues. This has the potential to revolutionize the way businesses interact with their customers, making customer service faster, more efficient and more personalized.

In addition to its applications in business, ChatGPT is also expected to play a major role in the field of education. By automating tedious and repetitive tasks, ChatGPT can free up teachers and instructors to focus on delivering personalized, high-quality instruction to students. This has the potential to improve student outcomes and reduce the burden on educators, helping to close the achievement gap and ensure that all students have access to high-quality education.

Another exciting possibility of ChatGPT is its ability to process and understand multiple languages. This opens up new opportunities for businesses to expand into new markets and reach new audiences, while also making it easier for individuals to communicate with people from all over the world. With the ability to translate text and speech in real-time, ChatGPT is set to play a major role in breaking down language barriers and enabling people from different cultures and backgrounds to connect and collaborate like never before.

Finally, ChatGPT is also expected to have a major impact on the field of creative writing. By providing writers with the ability to generate and refine new ideas and plot lines in real-time, ChatGPT has the potential to revolutionize the way that stories are written and help writers to create more engaging, complex and captivating works of fiction.

The integration of ChatGPT in virtual and augmented reality

As the world continues to evolve and technology advances, it's no surprise that ChatGPT has found a way to make its mark in the world of virtual and augmented reality. The integration of this cutting-edge language model with virtual and augmented reality has the potential to change the way we interact with technology and each other.

Virtual reality, or VR, refers to a computer-generated simulation of a three-dimensional environment that can be interacted with in a seemingly real or physical way. Augmented reality, or AR, involves the integration of virtual elements into the real world, providing users with a mixed reality experience. Both VR and AR have the potential to completely change the way we learn, work, and play, and ChatGPT is playing a key role in this transformation.

ChatGPT's natural language processing capabilities, combined with its ability to understand context and generate relevant responses, make it a valuable tool for VR and AR applications. By allowing users to interact with virtual environments in a conversational manner, ChatGPT is enhancing the overall experience and making it more intuitive.

For example, in the education sector, ChatGPT-powered VR and AR can offer students an interactive and engaging way to learn, providing them with hands-on experiences in a safe and controlled environment. In a virtual history lesson, students can use ChatGPT to interact with virtual historical figures, asking them questions and learning more about the past in a fun and interactive way.

In the healthcare industry, ChatGPT-powered VR and AR can be used to train medical professionals, allowing them to practice procedures in a virtual environment before performing them on real patients. This can help reduce the risk of errors and improve patient outcomes.

In the entertainment industry, ChatGPT-powered VR and AR can offer users a new level of immersion, allowing them to interact with virtual characters in a realistic and natural way. For example, in a VR game, users can use ChatGPT to converse with characters and make decisions that affect the outcome of the game.

ChatGPT's integration with VR and AR also has the potential to revolutionize the way we work. In virtual meetings, attendees can use ChatGPT to converse with each other in real-time, eliminating the need for physical meetings and making it easier to collaborate with people from around the world. In virtual coworking spaces, employees can use ChatGPT to interact with each other and complete tasks in a virtual environment, making remote work more efficient and enjoyable.

One of the key benefits of using ChatGPT in virtual and augmented reality is that it can help to eliminate the need for complex controllers and inputs. For example, instead of using a physical controller to move a virtual object, users can simply speak commands to ChatGPT and the AI will interpret and execute those commands in real-time. This could greatly simplify the user experience and make virtual and augmented reality more accessible to a wider range of people.

Another potential application of ChatGPT in virtual and augmented reality is in the field of education. By incorporating ChatGPT into virtual learning environments, educators can create interactive, engaging lessons that allow students to explore and learn in a virtual world. ChatGPT can also help to create more personalized learning experiences, as the AI can adjust its responses and interactions based on the individual needs and abilities of each student.

As technology continues to advance, virtual and augmented reality (VR and AR) are becoming more and more prevalent in our daily lives. From gaming to education and beyond, VR and AR are changing the way we interact with the world around us. And with the advent of ChatGPT, the integration of AI into these emerging technologies is becoming even more exciting.

ChatGPT can be used to create highly realistic and interactive virtual environments, where users can communicate with AI-powered characters, participate in virtual events, and even experience the world in a completely new way. For example, a VR game could use ChatGPT to generate in-game dialogue for characters, making them seem more lifelike and believable. This could result in a more immersive and engaging gaming experience for players.

In the realm of education, ChatGPT can be used to create AR-based learning tools that enhance the educational experience. For instance, an AR-powered textbook could use ChatGPT to provide additional context and information to students as they read, making the learning process more engaging and interactive.

Additionally, ChatGPT can be integrated into VR and AR for business applications, such as virtual trade shows, remote training, and virtual product demonstrations. With the help of ChatGPT, businesses can create interactive and highly-realistic virtual environments that allow them to engage with customers and employees in a more meaningful way.

As the integration of ChatGPT into VR and AR continues to evolve, the potential applications and benefits of this technology will only continue to grow. With its ability to create lifelike AI characters and provide real-time data and analysis, ChatGPT has the potential to transform the way we interact with virtual and augmented environments.

Understanding the capabilities of ChatGPT

ChatGPT is a highly advanced language processing system that has the ability to understand and generate human-like text. Developed by OpenAI, ChatGPT is part of a new generation of artificial intelligence technologies that is changing the way we interact with information and each other. But what exactly makes ChatGPT so unique and powerful? In this chapter, we'll explore the capabilities of ChatGPT and what sets it apart from other language processing systems.

One of the key capabilities of ChatGPT is its ability to generate human-like text. This is achieved through the use of deep learning algorithms and large amounts of training data. By processing this data, ChatGPT is able to learn the patterns and structures of human language, which allows it to generate text that is highly similar to that of a human. This makes ChatGPT a valuable tool for tasks such as language translation, content creation, and customer service, where natural language is critical.

Another key capability of ChatGPT is its ability to understand context. Unlike traditional language processing systems, ChatGPT is able to understand the context in which a piece of text is being used. This allows it to provide more accurate and relevant responses to questions and requests, which greatly improves its overall effectiveness. For example, if a user asks a question about a specific topic, ChatGPT will be able to understand the context of the question and provide a more accurate response based on that context.

ChatGPT also has the ability to understand and interpret emotions. This is achieved through the use of natural language processing techniques and machine learning algorithms that are trained to identify patterns and structures in text that indicate emotions. This allows ChatGPT to understand the tone and sentiment of a piece of text, which can be extremely useful in customer service and support applications, where understanding the emotions of customers is critical.

Another important capability of ChatGPT is its ability to handle large amounts of data. With its advanced algorithms and processing capabilities, ChatGPT can process and analyze large amounts of data quickly and accurately. This makes it an ideal solution for businesses and organizations looking to streamline their processes and increase efficiency. For example, ChatGPT can be used to process and analyze large data sets in real-time, which can provide valuable insights and help organizations make more informed decisions.

One of the key features of ChatGPT is its ability to converse naturally. ChatGPT has been trained on large amounts of data that includes natural language conversations, so it is able to generate text that resembles human-like speech. This means that when interacting with ChatGPT, users are able to engage in back-and-forth conversations that feel natural and effortless.

Another feature of ChatGPT is its ability to handle multiple tasks. Unlike traditional language processing systems that are only able to perform a single task, ChatGPT is able to perform a wide range of language-related tasks such as question answering, summarization, and language translation. This makes ChatGPT a versatile tool that can be used for a variety of applications, including customer service and support, content creation, and data analysis.

Another aspect that sets ChatGPT apart is its ability to learn and improve over time. ChatGPT is a deep learning model that is able to continuously improve its performance through exposure to new data. As users interact with ChatGPT, it is able to learn from their conversations and make adjustments to its algorithms, which helps it to provide more accurate and relevant responses.

Another important feature of ChatGPT is its ability to understand the intent behind a user's request. This is achieved through the use of advanced natural language processing techniques that allow ChatGPT to understand the underlying meaning behind a user's text. This makes it possible for ChatGPT to provide accurate responses to user requests, even when those requests are complex or contain multiple sub-requests.

Finally, ChatGPT is also highly scalable and efficient. With its advanced algorithms and processing capabilities, ChatGPT is able to handle large amounts of data and perform multiple tasks simultaneously. This makes it an ideal solution for businesses and organizations looking to streamline their processes and increase efficiency.

ChatGPT and its impact on society

The rise of ChatGPT has had a profound impact on society, revolutionizing the way we interact with technology and changing the way we think about the role of artificial intelligence in our lives. From customer service and support, to content creation and data analysis, ChatGPT has proven to be a valuable tool that can help individuals and organizations achieve their goals in new and innovative ways.

One of the most notable impacts of ChatGPT has been in the area of customer service and support. With its ability to converse naturally and understand user intent, ChatGPT has made it possible for businesses to provide 24/7 support to their customers, regardless of their location or time zone. This has made it easier for businesses to build strong relationships with their customers and provide high-quality support, even in the face of rapidly changing customer needs and expectations.

Another impact of ChatGPT has been in the realm of content creation. With its advanced language processing capabilities, ChatGPT has made it possible for users to generate high-quality content quickly and efficiently, without the need for extensive writing skills or knowledge of a particular subject. This has been especially beneficial for small businesses and individual entrepreneurs who previously struggled to create content that was engaging and relevant to their audience.

The rise of ChatGPT has also had a significant impact on the field of data analysis. With its ability to process large amounts of data and perform multiple tasks simultaneously, ChatGPT has made it easier for organizations to gain insights into complex data sets and make informed decisions based on that data. This has been particularly valuable in industries such as finance and healthcare, where the ability to quickly and accurately process large amounts of data can have a major impact on outcomes.

In addition to these practical applications, ChatGPT has also challenged our thinking about the role of artificial intelligence in society. As ChatGPT continues to evolve and improve, it raises important questions about what it means to be human and what role AI will play in shaping our future. It has also sparked debates about the ethics of using AI in certain contexts, such as the potential for AI to perpetuate biases or manipulate users.

Despite these challenges, the rise of ChatGPT has been a positive development for society overall. It has made it possible for individuals and organizations to achieve their goals in new and innovative ways, and has opened up new avenues for growth and discovery. As ChatGPT continues to evolve, it will likely have an even greater impact on society, helping us to solve complex problems and make our lives easier and more fulfilling.

ChatGPT and its impact on future

The impact of ChatGPT on the future is immense and far-reaching. As the technology continues to evolve and improve, it has the potential to revolutionize a wide range of industries and change the way we live our lives. In this chapter, we will explore some of the ways in which ChatGPT is likely to shape our future and the impact it will have on society as a whole.

One of the most exciting and impactful ways in which ChatGPT is likely to shape the future is by making information more accessible. With its advanced language processing capabilities, ChatGPT has the potential to help people find the information they need more easily, no matter where they are or what they are looking for. This could have a major impact on fields such as education and healthcare, where access to accurate and up-to-date information is critical.

Another important impact of ChatGPT on the future is its potential to improve productivity. As ChatGPT becomes more advanced and capable of handling a wider range of tasks, it has the potential to automate many routine and repetitive tasks, freeing up time and resources for more creative and meaningful work. This could have a major impact on the job market and the way we work, and could also help to boost economic growth and prosperity.

The rise of ChatGPT also has the potential to transform the way we communicate and interact with one another. With its ability to understand natural language and respond in a conversational manner, ChatGPT has the potential to become a critical tool for bridging linguistic and cultural barriers. This could have a major impact on fields such as international business and diplomacy, where effective communication is critical for success.

In addition to these practical applications, ChatGPT also has the potential to change the way we think about the role of artificial intelligence in our lives. As ChatGPT continues to evolve and improve, it is likely to raise important questions about the ethics of using AI and the potential consequences of relying too heavily on AI to make decisions and solve problems. This could lead to a wider discussion about the appropriate use of AI in society and the importance of ensuring that AI is developed and used in a responsible and ethical manner.

The rise of ChatGPT is also likely to have a major impact on the job market and the way we work. As ChatGPT becomes more capable of handling a wider range of tasks, it has the potential to automate many jobs that are currently performed by humans. This could lead to major changes in the job market, as workers will need to acquire new skills and adapt to new job roles in order to stay competitive.

Despite these challenges, the rise of ChatGPT is ultimately a positive development for society. With its ability to make information more accessible, improve productivity, and change the way we communicate and interact with one another, ChatGPT has the potential to transform the way we live our lives and make our world a better place. As we look to the future, it is clear that ChatGPT is poised to play a major role in shaping our world and helping us to achieve our goals in new and innovative ways.

Another important aspect of ChatGPT's impact on the future is its potential to improve customer service and support. With its advanced language processing capabilities, ChatGPT can help businesses to provide more efficient and effective support to their customers. This can help to improve customer satisfaction, reduce wait times, and increase customer loyalty, all of which are critical factors for the success of any business.

Additionally, ChatGPT has the potential to improve decision-making and problem-solving in various industries. By providing quick and accurate answers to complex questions, ChatGPT can help businesses to make better and more informed decisions. This can lead to improved operational efficiency and cost savings, as well as better outcomes for customers and clients.

Another area where ChatGPT is likely to have a major impact is in the field of personal assistants and virtual assistants. With its advanced language processing capabilities, ChatGPT has the potential to provide highly personalized and tailored assistance to individuals. This can help to save time and streamline various tasks and activities, such as scheduling appointments, ordering food, or finding information.

Moreover, ChatGPT has the potential to revolutionize the field of entertainment. With its ability to generate engaging and creative content, ChatGPT has the potential to become an important tool for artists, writers, and filmmakers. This could lead to the creation of new and innovative forms of entertainment, as well as new and more immersive experiences for audiences.

Another important aspect of ChatGPT's impact on the future is its potential to improve accessibility and inclusiveness. With its advanced language processing capabilities, ChatGPT has the potential to help people with disabilities or limited language proficiency to better access information and engage with the world around them. This could have a major impact on fields such as education, healthcare, and employment, helping to create a more inclusive and equitable society.

Finally, it's worth noting that the impact of ChatGPT on the future is likely to be influenced by the development of related technologies, such as natural language processing and machine learning. As these technologies continue to evolve and improve, they will likely play a critical role in shaping the future of ChatGPT and its impact on society.

ChatGPT and its impact on jobs in the future

The impact of ChatGPT on jobs in the future is a highly debated topic, with some experts predicting that the technology will lead to significant job loss, while others believe that it will create new and more lucrative job opportunities. To understand the full impact of ChatGPT on the job market, it's important to consider both the potential risks and benefits of this technology.

One of the main concerns about ChatGPT and its impact on jobs is that it has the potential to automate many tasks that were previously performed by humans. For example, ChatGPT could be used to automate customer service and support, replace data entry and administrative tasks, or even replace certain aspects of professional roles such as journalism or legal analysis. This could lead to significant job losses in a variety of industries, particularly for workers in low-skilled or repetitive jobs.

However, it's important to note that the impact of technology on jobs is not always straightforward. In many cases, the automation of certain tasks can lead to the creation of new job opportunities, particularly in fields such as technology, software development, and data analysis. For example, the development of ChatGPT is likely to create new jobs in areas such as programming, data science, and machine learning, which are highly in-demand and offer high salaries.

Additionally, ChatGPT has the potential to improve the quality of life for workers in a variety of industries. By automating routine and repetitive tasks, ChatGPT could free up workers to focus on more creative and fulfilling aspects of their jobs. This could lead to increased job satisfaction, reduced stress, and improved mental health, all of which are critical factors for the well-being of workers.

Another important aspect of ChatGPT's impact on jobs in the future is its potential to transform the way work is done. With its ability to provide quick and accurate answers to complex questions, ChatGPT has the potential to streamline and improve many aspects of work, such as research, problem-solving, and decision-making. This could lead to improved productivity and efficiency, as well as better outcomes for businesses and workers.

Moreover, ChatGPT has the potential to improve access to education and training, helping workers to stay up-to-date with the latest skills and technologies. By providing personalized and tailored assistance, ChatGPT could help individuals to acquire new skills and knowledge more quickly and efficiently. This could lead to improved career prospects and better outcomes for workers in a variety of industries.

It's worth noting that the impact of ChatGPT on jobs in the future will also be influenced by government policies and regulations. For example, policies that support worker retraining and education could help to mitigate the negative impact of job losses due to automation, while policies that support the development of new technologies could help to create new job opportunities.

Another aspect to consider when it comes to ChatGPT and its impact on jobs in the future is the ethics and implications of using AI in the workplace. As ChatGPT becomes more advanced and widespread, there are important questions to be addressed regarding its impact on worker privacy, autonomy, and accountability.

For example, the use of ChatGPT in the workplace could lead to increased surveillance of worker behavior and communication. This raises important privacy concerns and could impact worker trust and morale. Additionally, the use of ChatGPT could lead to an increased reliance on technology, potentially reducing the need for human workers and making it easier for companies to outsource jobs to other countries.

It's also important to consider the potential for ChatGPT to perpetuate bias and discrimination in the workplace. The algorithms that power ChatGPT are only as unbiased as the data they are trained on, and if the training data contains any biases, these biases could be reflected in the technology's outputs. This could result in discrimination against certain groups of workers, such as those with disabilities, women, or members of minority groups.

On the other hand, ChatGPT also has the potential to improve diversity and equality in the workplace. For example, the technology could help to eliminate human biases in hiring and promotion decisions, making it easier for underrepresented groups to secure jobs and advance in their careers. Additionally, ChatGPT could help to bridge language and cultural barriers, making it easier for workers from different backgrounds to communicate and collaborate effectively.

Ultimately, the impact of ChatGPT on jobs in the future will depend on how the technology is designed, implemented, and regulated. It will be important for companies and policymakers to consider the ethics and implications of using AI in the workplace, and to work to ensure that the benefits of this technology are shared by all. By doing so, we can ensure that ChatGPT has a positive impact on jobs and the future of work.

The future of AI and ChatGPT

The future of AI and ChatGPT is both exciting and uncertain. On the one hand, advances in AI technology promise to bring about major improvements in our lives, from faster and more accurate decision-making to the development of new and innovative products and services. On the other hand, the rapid pace of technological change raises important questions about the future of work and the impact of AI on society as a whole.

One of the most promising areas for the future of AI and ChatGPT is in the field of healthcare. AI-powered technologies like ChatGPT have the potential to revolutionize the way we diagnose and treat disease, helping to improve patient outcomes and reduce healthcare costs. For example, ChatGPT could be used to analyze vast amounts of medical data, providing doctors with real-time insights and recommendations based on the latest research and medical practices. This could lead to faster, more accurate diagnoses and more effective treatments, improving patient outcomes and saving lives.

Another area where AI and ChatGPT are likely to have a major impact is in the realm of transportation. With the advent of self-driving cars and other autonomous vehicles, AI is poised to play a key role in revolutionizing the way we move people and goods. ChatGPT could be used to power these vehicles, providing real-time decision-making and route optimization based on traffic patterns and other factors. This could lead to safer, more efficient transportation systems, reducing accidents, congestion, and emissions and improving the quality of life for people around the world.

Of course, the future of AI and ChatGPT also raises important ethical and social concerns. One of the biggest concerns is the potential for AI to automate many jobs and displace human workers. As AI technologies continue to advance, it's possible that a significant portion of the workforce could be replaced by machines, leading to mass unemployment and a widening income gap between those who are able to adapt to the new technological landscape and those who are not.

To mitigate these risks and ensure that the benefits of AI and ChatGPT are shared by all, it will be important for policymakers to take an active role in shaping the future of AI. This could include providing education and training programs to help workers transition to new jobs, investing in research and development to spur technological innovation, and regulating the use of AI to ensure that it is used in a responsible and ethical manner.

Another important aspect of the future of AI and ChatGPT is the role that it will play in advancing scientific discovery and innovation. With its ability to analyze vast amounts of data and make predictions based on that data, ChatGPT has the potential to revolutionize many fields, from medicine and biology to astronomy and physics.

For example, ChatGPT could be used to analyze large sets of genomic data, helping scientists to better understand the underlying causes of diseases and develop new treatments. It could also be used to model complex systems, such as the behavior of populations or the movement of particles in a fluid, helping scientists to gain new insights and make new discoveries.

In addition, AI and ChatGPT are also likely to play a major role in the development of new products and services. Companies and entrepreneurs are already using AI to create everything from intelligent personal assistants to self-driving cars, and this trend is only set to continue in the years ahead. As AI becomes more advanced and more accessible, we can expect to see a growing number of businesses leveraging its power to create new and innovative products and services that improve our lives and drive economic growth.

However, as with any rapidly advancing technology, there are also challenges that must be addressed in order to ensure that the benefits of AI and ChatGPT are realized. One of these challenges is ensuring that the algorithms used to drive AI systems are free from bias and discrimination. This is particularly important in fields like criminal justice, where decisions made by AI systems could have life-altering consequences for individuals and communities.

To address these and other challenges, it will be important for policymakers, businesses, and researchers to work together to promote responsible and ethical AI practices. This could include developing new standards and guidelines for the use of AI, investing in research to better understand the social and ethical implications of AI, and promoting transparency and accountability in the development and deployment of AI systems.

ChatGPT and its potential applications

The potential applications of ChatGPT are virtually limitless, as it has the ability to analyze vast amounts of data and make predictions based on that data. Here are just a few of the ways that ChatGPT is already being used and the many other ways it could be used in the future.

Customer Service: ChatGPT is already being used to power customer service chatbots that help customers quickly and easily get the information they need. These chatbots can be used by companies to provide 24/7 support, reducing wait times and improving the overall customer experience.

Healthcare: In the healthcare industry, ChatGPT could be used to analyze medical records and provide doctors and nurses with valuable insights into patient health and treatment options. This could lead to faster diagnoses and more effective treatments, ultimately improving patient outcomes.

Finance: In the finance industry, ChatGPT could be used to analyze stock market data and make predictions about future market trends. This could help traders and investors make more informed decisions, leading to better investment outcomes.

Retail: In the retail industry, ChatGPT could be used to analyze sales data and make recommendations to customers based on their shopping habits and preferences. This could help retailers provide a more personalized shopping experience and drive sales.

Education: In the education industry, ChatGPT could be used to provide personalized learning experiences for students. For example, ChatGPT could analyze a student's test scores, reading level, and other data to provide customized lesson plans and recommendations for learning resources.

Transportation: In the transportation industry, ChatGPT could be used to analyze traffic data and make predictions about traffic patterns and congestion. This could help city planners and transportation companies make better decisions about how to allocate resources and improve the overall efficiency of transportation systems.

Energy: In the energy industry, ChatGPT could be used to analyze energy usage data and make predictions about future energy demand. This could help energy companies better plan for future energy needs and make more informed decisions about energy production and distribution.

Another aspect to consider with ChatGPT and its potential applications is the development of Natural Language Processing (NLP). NLP is the technology behind ChatGPT's ability to understand and respond to human language in a conversational manner. As NLP continues to evolve, we can expect to see even more advanced and sophisticated ChatGPT systems that are capable of more nuanced and human-like conversations.

This has the potential to revolutionize the way we interact with technology and could lead to the development of new and innovative applications. For example, imagine being able to have a natural and intuitive conversation with your smart home devices, or being able to receive real-time language translation while traveling in a foreign country.

Another important aspect to consider is the role of ChatGPT in the development of the Internet of Things (IoT). The IoT refers to the interconnected network of physical devices, vehicles, buildings, and other items that are embedded with sensors, software, and network connectivity. With ChatGPT, these devices could be connected and able to communicate with one another, creating a truly smart and connected world.

For example, imagine your smart home devices being able to communicate with each other to optimize energy usage and reduce waste. Or, imagine your car being able to communicate with other vehicles on the road to improve traffic flow and reduce congestion. The possibilities are endless, and as the IoT continues to grow, ChatGPT will play a critical role in making this a reality.

In addition to these applications, ChatGPT has the potential to revolutionize the way we work and do business. For example, ChatGPT could be used to automate repetitive tasks and free up human workers to focus on more complex and creative tasks. This has the potential to increase productivity and efficiency, while also reducing the risk of burnout and job dissatisfaction.

These are just a few of the many potential applications of ChatGPT, and as the technology continues to evolve, we can expect to see many more innovative uses of this powerful tool.

However, as with any rapidly advancing technology, there are also challenges that must be addressed in order to ensure that the benefits of ChatGPT are realized. One of these challenges is ensuring that the algorithms used by ChatGPT are free from bias and discrimination. This is particularly important in fields like healthcare and finance, where decisions made by ChatGPT could have serious consequences for individuals and communities.

To address these and other challenges, it will be important for policymakers, businesses, and researchers to work together to promote responsible and ethical AI practices. This could include developing new standards and guidelines for the use of AI, investing in research to better understand the social and ethical implications of AI, and promoting transparency and accountability in the development and deployment of AI systems.

The benefits and limitations of ChatGPT

The benefits and limitations of ChatGPT are an important consideration when evaluating its potential impact on our lives and the world we live in. On one hand, ChatGPT offers numerous benefits that have the potential to transform the way we interact with technology, work, and do business. On the other hand, there are also limitations to be aware of, which may impact its effectiveness and adoption in certain scenarios.

One of the key benefits of ChatGPT is its ability to automate repetitive and mundane tasks, freeing up human workers to focus on more complex and creative tasks. This has the potential to increase productivity and efficiency, while also reducing the risk of burnout and job dissatisfaction. For example, ChatGPT could be used to handle customer service inquiries, freeing up human customer service representatives to focus on more complex and challenging issues.

Another benefit of ChatGPT is its ability to provide quick and accurate information to users. With its advanced Natural Language Processing (NLP) capabilities, ChatGPT is able to understand and respond to human language in a conversational manner, making it a valuable tool for retrieving information and answering questions. This has the potential to improve accessibility to information and knowledge, making it easier for people to find the information they need when they need it.

However, despite these benefits, there are also limitations to be aware of when it comes to ChatGPT. One such limitation is its current limitations in understanding context and tone. While ChatGPT is capable of understanding and responding to human language, it may not always accurately interpret the context or tone of a conversation. This can result in misunderstandings or inappropriate responses, which may impact the user experience.

Another limitation is the current limitations of NLP in understanding and processing non-standard language and accents. This may impact the accuracy of ChatGPT's responses in certain scenarios, such as when dealing with users who have non-standard accents or use non-standard language. This may also impact the effectiveness of ChatGPT in certain countries or regions where non-standard language and accents are more common.

In addition, there are also ethical considerations to be aware of when it comes to the use of ChatGPT. For example, there is the risk of ChatGPT being used to automate biased decision-making processes, or to spread misinformation and propaganda. These are important ethical considerations that need to be taken into account when evaluating the benefits and limitations of ChatGPT.

Another area where ChatGPT has the potential to have a significant impact is in education and learning. With its ability to understand and respond to human language, ChatGPT has the potential to provide personalized and interactive learning experiences, making education more accessible and engaging for students of all ages and abilities.

For example, ChatGPT could be used to provide real-time feedback and support to students as they work through learning materials. This has the potential to improve students' engagement and motivation, as well as helping them to identify and overcome learning challenges more quickly. Additionally, ChatGPT could also be used to personalize learning experiences based on students' individual strengths and weaknesses, providing a more effective and efficient learning experience.

However, there are also limitations to be aware of when it comes to the use of ChatGPT in education and learning. One such limitation is the current limitations of NLP in understanding and processing complex academic concepts and terminology. This may impact the accuracy of ChatGPT's responses in certain learning scenarios, such as when dealing with advanced academic subjects.

Another limitation is the risk of over-reliance on ChatGPT, leading to a reduction in critical thinking and problem-solving skills. If students become too reliant on ChatGPT for answers and solutions, they may lose the ability to think critically and independently, which is essential for success in both academic and professional settings.

Finally, there is also the ethical consideration of data privacy and security when it comes to the use of ChatGPT in education. With students providing personal information and data as part of their learning experiences, it is important to ensure that this data is protected and secure, to prevent unauthorized access or misuse.

Ethical considerations in the use of ChatGPT

The rapid advancement of artificial intelligence has brought about many exciting new possibilities, but it has also raised important ethical questions about the use and development of these technologies. The use of ChatGPT is no exception, and as the technology becomes more widespread, it is important to consider the ethical implications of its use.

One of the most significant ethical considerations with the use of ChatGPT is the issue of bias. The AI algorithms used in ChatGPT are trained on large amounts of data, and if that data is biased in any way, the AI may develop biases of its own. This could result in ChatGPT exhibiting prejudice or discrimination based on gender, race, religion, or other factors, which could have serious consequences for individuals and society as a whole.

Another ethical consideration is the issue of data privacy and security. With the increasing use of AI, there is a growing concern about the collection and storage of personal data, and the potential for misuse or abuse of this information. ChatGPT may be collecting and storing large amounts of personal data as part of its interactions with users, and it is important to ensure that this data is protected and used in a responsible and ethical manner.

Another ethical issue is the potential for AI to be used for malicious purposes. With its advanced language processing capabilities, ChatGPT has the potential to be used to spread misinformation or propaganda, to manipulate public opinion, or to carry out cyber attacks. It is important for organizations to be aware of these risks and to put in place measures to prevent these malicious uses of ChatGPT.

Another ethical consideration in the use of ChatGPT is accountability. With AI systems like ChatGPT, it can be difficult to determine who is responsible for any errors or negative outcomes that may result from its use. This is particularly relevant in situations where ChatGPT is used to make decisions that affect individuals, such as in healthcare or financial services. It is important to establish clear lines of accountability for AI systems, so that individuals have a clear understanding of who is responsible for any negative outcomes and can take action to seek redress if necessary.

Another issue to consider is transparency. AI systems like ChatGPT operate on complex algorithms and decision-making processes, which can be difficult for humans to understand and interpret. This can lead to a lack of transparency in the decision-making process, which can be problematic in situations where the outcomes of AI systems have significant implications for individuals or society. It is important for AI systems to be designed with transparency in mind, so that individuals can understand how decisions are being made and can hold organizations accountable for their actions.

In addition to these ethical considerations, it is also important to consider the regulatory framework surrounding the use of ChatGPT. With the increasing use of AI, there is a need for clear and consistent regulations that set standards for the use and development of these technologies. This could include regulations around data privacy, the use of AI in decision-making processes, and the impact of AI on employment and the job market.

Finally, it is important to consider the role of education and awareness in addressing the ethical considerations surrounding ChatGPT. With the rapid advancement of AI, it is important for individuals and organizations to be informed and educated about the benefits and risks associated with these technologies. This can help to ensure that individuals and organizations are better equipped to make informed decisions about the use of ChatGPT and to ensure that these technologies are used in a responsible and ethical manner.

The role of ChatGPT in education

The role of ChatGPT in education is one that has the potential to revolutionize the way that students learn and interact with technology. ChatGPT provides an interactive and engaging platform for students to explore and learn about a wide range of subjects, from science and mathematics to history and literature. This technology can be used to create personalized learning experiences that are tailored to the needs and interests of individual students, allowing them to progress at their own pace and on their own terms.

One of the key benefits of ChatGPT in education is its ability to provide instant feedback and support to students. By using natural language processing and machine learning, ChatGPT is able to understand and respond to students' questions in real-time, providing them with the information and guidance they need to succeed. This can be especially beneficial for students who struggle with certain subjects or who need extra support to grasp new concepts.

Another important aspect of ChatGPT in education is its ability to make learning more interactive and engaging. For example, ChatGPT can be used to create virtual classrooms or interactive lessons that bring subjects to life for students. This can help to foster a more dynamic and engaging learning environment, one that is better suited to the needs of the digital generation.

In addition to its role in providing support and engagement for students, ChatGPT also has the potential to play an important role in the assessment and evaluation of learning. By analyzing student interactions and performance over time, ChatGPT can provide valuable insights into student understanding and progress. This information can then be used to inform instruction and provide targeted support for students who need it most.

However, while the potential benefits of ChatGPT in education are clear, there are also a number of challenges and limitations that must be considered. For example, the technology is still in its early stages of development and there is a need for further research and development to fully realize its potential. Additionally, there is a need for greater awareness and understanding among teachers and students about the capabilities and limitations of ChatGPT, as well as the potential benefits and risks associated with its use.

Another important factor to consider is the potential impact of ChatGPT on the workforce and employment. As ChatGPT and other AI technologies become more advanced and more widely adopted, there is a risk that they may displace human workers in certain industries, particularly in areas such as customer service and support. This raises important questions about the future of work and the need for education and training programs that can help individuals adapt to the changing technological landscape.

The integration of ChatGPT and other AI technologies in education has the potential to revolutionize the way we learn and interact with information. One of the key benefits of using ChatGPT in education is its ability to provide personalized and instant feedback to students. This could greatly enhance the student's learning experience and make it easier for teachers to track student progress. ChatGPT can also be used as an educational tool to provide instant access to vast amounts of information, and to facilitate interaction between students and teachers, regardless of their physical location.

Another important aspect of using ChatGPT in education is its potential to promote creativity and critical thinking. By providing students with access to an array of data and information, ChatGPT can inspire them to ask questions, analyze data and develop new ideas. This could help to create a more engaging and participatory learning experience, and could foster a more innovative and entrepreneurial spirit among students.

However, it is important to note that there are also some limitations to the use of ChatGPT in education. For example, while ChatGPT can provide access to a vast amount of information, it may not always provide the most accurate or up-to-date information. Additionally, some experts have expressed concerns that relying on AI technologies like ChatGPT could lead to a decrease in critical thinking skills and independent thinking, as students become too dependent on instant answers and feedback.

Given these benefits and limitations, it is important for educators and policymakers to carefully consider the role that ChatGPT and other AI technologies should play in education. By doing so, we can ensure that these technologies are used to support learning and education, rather than becoming a hindrance to it. Ultimately, the goal should be to create an educational environment that fosters creativity, critical thinking, and independent thinking, while also providing students with the tools and resources they need to succeed in the modern world.

The future of human-robot interaction and ChatGPT

Human-robot interaction (HRI) is rapidly becoming an increasingly important field of study, as advancements in artificial intelligence and robotics continue to shape our future. ChatGPT, as a large language model developed by OpenAI, is playing a critical role in this field, by enabling robots and other AI-powered systems to engage in human-like conversation and communication. In this chapter, we will explore the future of human-robot interaction and the role that ChatGPT will play in shaping it.

One of the most exciting possibilities of human-robot interaction is the development of intelligent robots that can understand and respond to human emotions and social cues. In the future, we may see robots that are capable of engaging in human-like conversations, providing emotional support, and even forming social relationships with humans. ChatGPT, with its ability to generate human-like responses, will play a critical role in enabling this type of human-robot interaction.

Another important area of development in HRI is the use of robots in healthcare. In the future, robots powered by ChatGPT could assist doctors and other healthcare professionals in diagnosing and treating patients. These robots could provide instant access to vast amounts of medical information and knowledge, helping to ensure that patients receive the best possible care. Furthermore, ChatGPT could help robots to communicate more effectively with patients, providing them with information and support in a compassionate and empathetic manner.

The field of education is also likely to be impacted by HRI, as robots powered by ChatGPT become more prevalent in classrooms. These robots could provide instant access to information and educational resources, while also engaging students in interactive and engaging learning experiences. This could help to make education more accessible, particularly in remote and underdeveloped regions, and could also help to inspire students to pursue careers in science, technology, engineering, and mathematics.

One of the most important benefits of HRI is that it has the potential to greatly improve our quality of life. For example, robots powered by ChatGPT could assist the elderly and people with disabilities, providing them with support and care that would otherwise be difficult or impossible to obtain. In addition, ChatGPT could help robots to understand and respond to human emotions and social cues, helping to ensure that they are providing support and care in a compassionate and empathetic manner.

However, there are also some important ethical considerations that must be taken into account when developing HRI. For example, there are concerns about the potential for robots to be used in ways that are harmful to humans, such as in military or surveillance applications. Additionally, there are concerns about the potential for robots to be used to replace human workers, leading to job losses and economic inequality.

Given these benefits and limitations, it is clear that the future of human-robot interaction will be shaped by the development and use of ChatGPT and other AI technologies. As such, it is important for policymakers, researchers, and technology developers to consider the implications of this technology and to work together to ensure that it is used in ways that promote the welfare and well-being of all people. Whether through the development of intelligent robots that can engage in human-like conversations, or through the use of robots in healthcare and education, the future of HRI promises to be both exciting and challenging.

Human-robot interaction is a rapidly growing field with the advancement of technology and the increasing popularity of robotics. With the advent of language models such as ChatGPT, the way in which humans interact with robots is undergoing a significant change. In this chapter, we will delve into the future of human-robot interaction and how ChatGPT is set to play a crucial role.

One of the biggest advancements in human-robot interaction has been the development of conversational AI. With the help of language models like ChatGPT, robots are now able to understand and respond to human speech in a more natural and human-like manner. This is transforming the way in which robots interact with humans, making it easier and more intuitive for people to engage with them.

In the future, it is likely that human-robot interaction will become even more seamless and intuitive. ChatGPT and other language models will continue to evolve, allowing robots to understand more complex human speech and respond in a more sophisticated manner. Additionally, advancements in robotics technology will allow robots to interact with humans through more natural forms of communication, such as gestures and facial expressions.

One of the key benefits of human-robot interaction is that it has the potential to make life easier and more convenient for humans. For example, robots equipped with ChatGPT could be used in a variety of different settings, from homes and offices to hospitals and schools. They could perform tasks such as answering questions, scheduling appointments, and helping people with day-to-day tasks.

However, there are also some limitations and ethical considerations that must be taken into account. For example, it is important to ensure that robots equipped with ChatGPT are designed to operate in a safe and secure manner, and that they do not pose a threat to human safety. Additionally, there are concerns about the potential for robots to be used for malicious purposes, such as spreading false information or engaging in cyber attacks.

Despite these limitations, the future of human-robot interaction is incredibly exciting, and ChatGPT is set to play a significant role. As technology continues to advance, it is likely that we will see even more sophisticated and intuitive human-robot interactions in the future, which will revolutionize the way in which humans interact with technology and each other.

The role of ChatGPT in cybersecurity

As technology continues to advance and shape our world, the field of cybersecurity is becoming increasingly important. With the growing number of connected devices and the increasing amounts of sensitive information being stored and transmitted online, the potential for cyber attacks and data breaches has never been greater. In this context, ChatGPT has the potential to play a major role in helping to keep our digital lives and information safe.

One of the key ways that ChatGPT can contribute to cybersecurity is by helping to identify and stop cyber threats before they can cause harm. This is accomplished through the use of advanced algorithms and machine learning techniques, which allow ChatGPT to analyze vast amounts of data and identify patterns and anomalies that might indicate a security breach or attack. By constantly monitoring the digital landscape, ChatGPT can quickly detect and respond to emerging threats, providing organizations and individuals with an extra layer of protection against cybercrime.

In addition to its role in detecting and preventing cyber attacks, ChatGPT can also be used to help organizations and individuals better understand and manage their cyber risk. For example, ChatGPT can be integrated into risk management systems to provide real-time analysis of an organization's cyber security posture, helping decision-makers to identify areas of weakness and develop more effective risk mitigation strategies.

Another potential application of ChatGPT in the field of cybersecurity is in the area of fraud detection. With the growing use of online transactions and digital currencies, the risk of financial fraud has increased significantly. ChatGPT can be used to analyze large amounts of transaction data and identify patterns of suspicious behavior, helping to detect and prevent fraud before it can occur. This can help financial institutions and other organizations to reduce their exposure to fraud-related losses, and improve their overall level of cyber security.

The integration of artificial intelligence in the field of cybersecurity has proven to be a significant milestone in the tech industry. With the increase in the number of cyber attacks, it is crucial to have an advanced system that can prevent and detect malicious activities. ChatGPT, as an AI language model, has the potential to play a crucial role in enhancing cybersecurity. The vast amount of data that it has been trained on and its ability to process large amounts of information make it an ideal candidate for cyber threat analysis.

One of the areas where ChatGPT can be of great help is in the identification of phishing scams. Phishing scams are a major threat to online security, and they can result in significant financial losses. ChatGPT, with its ability to understand and analyze language patterns, can be used to detect phishing scams by identifying the anomalies in the language used in the emails or messages. This, in turn, will enable individuals and organizations to take appropriate action to prevent any potential losses.

Another area where ChatGPT can be utilized is in network security. ChatGPT can be trained to recognize and flag any unusual activities that may indicate a security breach. For example, ChatGPT can analyze log files from firewalls and intrusion detection systems, and identify patterns that may indicate an attack. This can help security teams to detect and respond to threats more quickly and efficiently, reducing the risk of data loss or theft.

In addition, ChatGPT can be used to improve the efficiency of incident response processes. ChatGPT can be trained to analyze and categorize security incidents, allowing security teams to prioritize and respond to the most critical incidents more quickly.

This will enable organizations to minimize the impact of a security breach and reduce the overall cost of incident response.

Another area where ChatGPT can make a significant impact is in the field of threat intelligence. Threat intelligence is the process of collecting and analyzing information about potential cyber threats. ChatGPT can be trained to identify and analyze large amounts of threat intelligence data, making it easier for security teams to stay up-to-date with the latest threats. This will enable organizations to proactively protect themselves against cyber attacks, reducing the risk of a breach.

ChatGPT's ability to generate creative content

The ability of ChatGPT to generate creative content is one of the most exciting and potentially transformative aspects of the technology. While artificial intelligence has been used in various forms of content creation for decades, the advent of cutting-edge language models like ChatGPT marks a new era in the field. The technology's ability to generate text, images, music, and more, with a level of sophistication that can sometimes rival that of human creators, is changing the way we think about creativity and art.

One of the most remarkable things about ChatGPT is its ability to generate content that is not only factually accurate, but also emotionally engaging. This has far-reaching implications for a variety of industries, including advertising, entertainment, and media. For example, advertisers can use ChatGPT to generate eye-catching product descriptions and advertisements that resonate with their target audience. This not only increases the chances of a successful marketing campaign, but also helps brands to better understand their customers' wants and needs.

In the entertainment industry, ChatGPT has already shown its potential to revolutionize the way stories are created and told. With its ability to generate entire scenes and dialogues, it has the potential to change the way films, TV shows, and video games are produced. The technology can also be used to generate music and sound effects, making it a valuable tool for musicians and audio engineers.

Another exciting application of ChatGPT's content-creation capabilities is in the field of virtual and augmented reality. ChatGPT's ability to generate detailed 3D environments and characters can help bring virtual worlds to life in ways that were previously impossible. The technology can also be used to generate lifelike simulations of real-world environments, making it a valuable tool for architects, urban planners, and others who are working to create more livable, sustainable communities.

Despite all of these exciting possibilities, there are also concerns about the potential limitations and drawbacks of using ChatGPT to generate creative content. One concern is that the technology may be used to create content that is misleading or even harmful. For example, ChatGPT could be used to create fake news stories or false information that is spread on social media, with potentially disastrous consequences. Additionally, there are concerns about the impact that ChatGPT-generated content could have on the job market, particularly for creative professionals who may see their livelihoods threatened by the technology.

Despite these challenges, the future of creative content generation with ChatGPT is bright. As the technology continues to improve and evolve, it has the potential to transform the way we think about creativity and art, and to bring about a new era of innovation in content creation. Whether the future will bring more opportunities or challenges for creative professionals remains to be seen, but one thing is clear: the impact of ChatGPT on the field of content creation will be far-reaching and profound.

The idea of a machine generating creative content might have seemed impossible a few decades ago, but with the rapid advancements in Artificial Intelligence, it is now a reality. ChatGPT, a state-of-the-art language model developed by OpenAI, has the ability to generate a wide range of creative content, from poetry and fiction to music and visual art.

While some may argue that creativity is a uniquely human quality, ChatGPT has proven that it can generate content that is not only impressive but also captivating. With its advanced language processing capabilities, it can create articles, stories, and poems that are coherent, compelling, and often indistinguishable from human-created content. In fact, some creative works generated by ChatGPT have even been published in literary magazines and anthologies.

Moreover, the ability of ChatGPT to learn and adapt to different styles, genres, and forms of creative expression has further enhanced its ability to generate content that is not only diverse but also innovative. This makes ChatGPT an invaluable tool for writers, artists, and other creative professionals who are looking to expand their artistic horizons and experiment with new forms of expression.

Aside from its potential to inspire new forms of creative expression, ChatGPT can also be used to automate certain aspects of the creative process. For example, it can be utilized to generate outlines, story summaries, and even entire scripts for films and TV shows. This not only saves time and effort for creative professionals but also opens up new possibilities for the entertainment industry.

However, despite its impressive capabilities, it is important to note that ChatGPT is not a replacement for human creativity. While it can generate content that is aesthetically pleasing and thought-provoking, it lacks the emotional depth, personal experiences, and unique perspectives that are the hallmarks of human-created content. Additionally, while it can generate content that is technically sound, it lacks the human touch that is so essential to great creative works.

The integration of ChatGPT in autonomous systems

Autonomous systems refer to technology that operates without the need for human intervention. These systems are designed to work on their own, using artificial intelligence, machine learning, and other advanced technologies to make decisions, process information, and perform tasks. ChatGPT, with its powerful language processing abilities, has the potential to greatly enhance the functionality of autonomous systems.

One area where ChatGPT can be particularly beneficial is in the development of autonomous vehicles. ChatGPT can be integrated into the vehicle's control system to provide real-time information and make decisions based on that information. For example, ChatGPT can analyze traffic patterns, road conditions, and weather conditions to determine the best route for the vehicle to take. This could help improve the safety and efficiency of autonomous vehicles and reduce the risk of accidents.

Another area where ChatGPT can play a role in autonomous systems is in the development of intelligent virtual assistants. These systems can use ChatGPT to understand and respond to user requests in natural language, making the interactions more intuitive and human-like. This can lead to a more seamless and enjoyable experience for users, which is particularly important in industries such as healthcare, where virtual assistants are being used to provide patient care.

In the field of home automation, ChatGPT can also play a key role in developing autonomous systems that can perform a range of tasks such as controlling lighting, temperature, and security systems. ChatGPT can use natural language processing to understand and respond to user requests, making the interaction more natural and user-friendly. This can greatly enhance the functionality of home automation systems and make them more accessible to a wider range of users.

The integration of ChatGPT into autonomous systems can also have significant implications for the future of work. As ChatGPT becomes more advanced and capable of performing a wider range of tasks, it could lead to the automation of many jobs that were previously performed by humans. This could result in significant job losses, but it could also lead to the creation of new jobs in areas such as the development and maintenance of autonomous systems.

As the field of artificial intelligence continues to evolve, the integration of ChatGPT into autonomous systems is becoming increasingly relevant. Autonomous systems refer to technological systems that can perform tasks without human intervention. These systems range from autonomous vehicles to industrial robots, and they have the potential to revolutionize the way we live and work.

The integration of ChatGPT into autonomous systems offers several benefits. Firstly, ChatGPT's ability to understand and process human language makes it an ideal candidate for controlling and communicating with autonomous systems. For example, a driver could give voice commands to an autonomous vehicle powered by ChatGPT, making the driving experience more convenient and intuitive. In industrial settings, ChatGPT could be used to communicate with robots and other autonomous systems, enabling them to carry out tasks more efficiently and effectively.

Another potential benefit of ChatGPT's integration into autonomous systems is improved safety. Autonomous systems can be programmed to follow strict safety protocols, and ChatGPT can help ensure that these protocols are followed correctly. For example, ChatGPT could be used to monitor autonomous vehicles for any signs of malfunction, and take action to prevent accidents. In industrial settings, ChatGPT could monitor robots to ensure that they are operating within safe parameters, and intervene if necessary to prevent accidents.

However, there are also some limitations to the integration of ChatGPT into autonomous systems. One of the biggest limitations is the cost of developing and implementing these systems. Autonomous systems are complex and require significant investment in research and development. In addition, there may also be concerns about the reliability and accuracy of ChatGPT's outputs, especially in critical applications such as autonomous vehicles.

Another important consideration is the ethical implications of using ChatGPT in autonomous systems. For example, who is responsible if an autonomous vehicle powered by ChatGPT causes an accident? There are also concerns about the privacy implications of using ChatGPT in autonomous systems, as well as the potential for the technology to be misused.

ChatGPT's impact on human language and linguistic diversity

The rise of artificial intelligence and machine learning has revolutionized the way we process, understand, and produce language. One of the most remarkable products of this technological revolution is ChatGPT, an AI-powered conversational model developed by OpenAI. ChatGPT has been trained on a massive corpus of text data and has the ability to generate human-like responses to a wide range of questions and prompts.

But as ChatGPT continues to gain traction and impact the world of technology, its impact on human language and linguistic diversity also deserves closer examination. In this chapter, we'll explore the ways in which ChatGPT is changing the way we use and think about language, and examine both the potential benefits and limitations of this AI tool.

One of the primary ways in which ChatGPT is affecting human language is by improving our ability to communicate with computers. ChatGPT is designed to respond to natural language input, meaning that users can communicate with it in much the same way they would with another person. This has the potential to make technology more accessible and user-friendly, especially for those who may not be tech-savvy. By allowing us to interact with computers using the language we use every day, ChatGPT is helping to bridge the gap between human and machine communication.

However, this close interaction between human and machine language also raises important questions about the role of natural language in the future. As ChatGPT continues to develop, it's possible that our use of language may begin to change in response to the way the AI model processes and understands language. For example, if ChatGPT is trained to understand specific language patterns, it may become more difficult for us to use language in creative or unconventional ways.

Another way in which ChatGPT is impacting human language is by enabling the creation of new and diverse forms of content. With its ability to generate written responses to prompts, ChatGPT has the potential to play a role in a wide range of creative applications, from writing fiction to composing poetry. This has the potential to open up new avenues for creative expression and experimentation, but it also raises questions about the role of human authorship in an age of AI-generated content.

The impact of ChatGPT on linguistic diversity is also a matter of concern. As the AI model is trained on massive amounts of text data, it may be more likely to reflect the language patterns and biases of its training data. This could lead to the reinforcement of existing linguistic hierarchies and the marginalization of minority languages and dialects.

It's important to remember that while ChatGPT is an impressive technological achievement, it is still only a tool. As with any tool, the way it is used and the impact it has will depend on the intentions and values of those who use it. It's up to us as a society to ensure that ChatGPT is used in a way that promotes linguistic diversity and preserves the rich cultural heritage embodied in human language.

The advancements in artificial intelligence and language processing technology have greatly impacted the way in which human language is understood, processed and utilized. With ChatGPT being at the forefront of these developments, it is worth exploring the impact it may have on human language and linguistic diversity.

ChatGPT is a language model that has been trained on massive amounts of text data and is capable of generating human-like responses. It has the ability to process and understand complex and nuanced language, and to produce responses that are grammatically and semantically coherent. This capability opens up a whole new world of possibilities for the field of language processing, and it will likely have a profound impact on the way in which human language is used in the future.

One of the most exciting applications of ChatGPT is in the field of language translation. With the ability to process large amounts of text data and generate coherent translations, ChatGPT has the potential to revolutionize the way in which people communicate with one another across linguistic and cultural boundaries. This would have far-reaching benefits for global commerce, diplomacy, and cultural exchange.

Another area in which ChatGPT could have a significant impact is in the field of language education. With its ability to process and understand complex linguistic structures, ChatGPT could be used to create intelligent language tutors that can provide personalized instruction and feedback to students of all levels. This could help to make language learning more accessible and effective, and could help to promote linguistic diversity by making it easier for people to learn new languages.

However, the increasing reliance on ChatGPT and other AI systems for language processing raises some important questions about the future of human language and linguistic diversity. There is a concern that as these systems become more prevalent, they may lead to a homogenization of language, with people relying more on machine-generated language and losing their ability to communicate effectively in their own languages. Additionally, there is a risk that the use of ChatGPT may further reinforce existing language inequalities, as the systems are only as good as the data they are trained on, and may not accurately represent the linguistic diversity of the world.

Despite these concerns, it is clear that ChatGPT and other AI systems have the potential to greatly enhance our ability to communicate and understand one another, and to promote linguistic diversity by making it easier for people to learn new languages. However, it will be important to ensure that these systems are developed and used in a responsible and ethical manner, so that their impact on human language and linguistic diversity is positive and beneficial.

The potential of ChatGPT for financial forecasting

In the world of finance and economics, accurate forecasting is crucial for success. The ability to predict future market trends and consumer behavior can give businesses and investors a significant advantage. With the increasing use of artificial intelligence, it's not surprising that ChatGPT has become an important tool in financial forecasting.

ChatGPT is a cutting-edge language model developed by OpenAI that has the ability to generate human-like responses and interact with users in natural language. This advanced technology has the potential to revolutionize the world of financial forecasting by providing businesses with more accurate and comprehensive data analysis.

One of the primary benefits of ChatGPT for financial forecasting is its ability to process large amounts of data in real-time. With its advanced natural language processing capabilities, ChatGPT can quickly analyze vast amounts of information and identify trends and patterns that would otherwise be overlooked. This speed and accuracy can provide businesses with a significant advantage in making well-informed investment decisions.

Another advantage of ChatGPT in financial forecasting is its ability to adapt and learn. As it interacts with users, it can continually improve its responses and predictions based on new data and insights. This ability to learn and evolve means that businesses can rely on ChatGPT for ongoing and up-to-date financial forecasting, providing them with a competitive advantage in an ever-changing market.

Despite its many benefits, there are also limitations to ChatGPT's use in financial forecasting. For example, the technology is still relatively new, and there may be unforeseen problems that arise as it is more widely adopted. Additionally, ChatGPT is dependent on the quality and accuracy of the data it is fed. If the data it uses is inaccurate or biased, this could impact the validity of its predictions.

Another consideration is the ethics of relying on artificial intelligence for financial forecasting. Some experts argue that relying on AI algorithms such as ChatGPT could lead to a loss of human expertise and decision-making, particularly in the financial industry. There are also concerns about the potential for bias and discrimination, as AI algorithms may perpetuate existing biases and perpetuate discriminatory practices if not monitored carefully.

Despite these limitations, the potential of ChatGPT for financial forecasting cannot be ignored. With its advanced natural language processing capabilities and ability to quickly analyze vast amounts of data, ChatGPT has the potential to revolutionize the world of financial forecasting and provide businesses with a significant competitive advantage. As AI continues to advance, it is likely that ChatGPT and other similar technologies will play an increasingly important role in the financial industry.

Financial forecasting is a crucial aspect of the financial industry and has significant implications for individuals and organizations alike. The use of technology has already revolutionized financial forecasting, with data analytics and machine learning algorithms becoming increasingly popular in recent years. However, the emergence of advanced language models such as ChatGPT has the potential to take financial forecasting to the next level.

One of the key benefits of using ChatGPT in financial forecasting is its ability to process vast amounts of data quickly and accurately. With its advanced natural language processing capabilities, ChatGPT can analyze large volumes of financial data, including financial reports, news articles, and social media posts, and provide highly accurate predictions about future market trends. This can help organizations make informed decisions about investments and risk management, leading to better outcomes for both investors and companies.

Another benefit of ChatGPT in financial forecasting is its ability to learn from its previous predictions. With its deep learning algorithms, ChatGPT can continually improve its predictions based on the accuracy of previous forecasts. This means that the more data it processes, the more accurate its predictions will become, making it a powerful tool for long-term financial forecasting.

However, it's important to note that the use of ChatGPT in financial forecasting is not without its limitations. For example, financial forecasting is inherently uncertain, and no amount of data processing or machine learning algorithms can guarantee 100% accuracy. Additionally, there are also concerns about the transparency of AI algorithms like ChatGPT, as it can be difficult to understand how they arrive at their predictions. This can lead to a lack of trust in the predictions and may limit their adoption by the financial industry.

The integration of ChatGPT in renewable energy solutions

Renewable energy has become a hot topic in recent years, with the world seeking to reduce its carbon footprint and find more sustainable energy sources. ChatGPT, a cutting-edge language processing AI system developed by OpenAI, has the potential to play a significant role in advancing the development of renewable energy solutions.

To understand the potential of ChatGPT in the renewable energy space, it is important to first understand the challenges facing the industry. Renewable energy sources such as wind, solar, and hydropower are dependent on weather conditions, making their output unpredictable and difficult to control. The development and implementation of large-scale renewable energy projects is also hindered by complex regulatory frameworks, as well as economic and political pressures.

Enter ChatGPT, which offers a number of advantages over traditional approaches to energy management. Its advanced language processing capabilities allow it to quickly analyze large amounts of data and extract relevant information, helping energy companies to more effectively evaluate and predict energy demand, supply, and costs. Additionally, ChatGPT's ability to quickly and accurately analyze vast amounts of information makes it an ideal tool for optimizing energy generation, storage, and distribution systems.

For example, ChatGPT could be used to monitor the output of wind and solar farms and provide real-time data on their performance, allowing energy companies to make more informed decisions about when and how much energy to generate and store. It could also be used to help renewable energy companies navigate complex regulatory requirements and understand the potential impact of proposed policy changes.

Another potential use case for ChatGPT in the renewable energy space is to assist in the development of new energy storage solutions. Renewable energy sources like wind and solar are dependent on weather conditions, which can result in sudden fluctuations in energy generation. Energy storage solutions are needed to help mitigate these fluctuations and ensure a stable and consistent energy supply. ChatGPT could help energy companies to analyze large amounts of data on energy generation and storage, identify patterns and trends, and develop new and innovative energy storage solutions.

Furthermore, ChatGPT could also play a role in advancing the development of smart grid systems, which aim to intelligently manage energy distribution networks. ChatGPT's ability to process large amounts of data in real-time could help energy companies to better understand and predict energy demand, enabling them to dynamically balance supply and demand to improve grid stability and reduce energy waste.

ChatGPT's impact on human knowledge and understanding

As technology advances, the world is constantly evolving and expanding, and with it, our understanding of the world around us. Artificial intelligence has been at the forefront of this technological revolution and is playing an increasingly crucial role in shaping our understanding of the world and the way we interact with it. One AI technology that has been making waves in recent years is ChatGPT, a conversational AI model developed by OpenAI. In this chapter, we will explore the impact that ChatGPT has had on human knowledge and understanding.

ChatGPT has the ability to process vast amounts of information, generate new ideas, and answer complex questions. This has made it a valuable tool for researchers, students, and others who are seeking to expand their understanding of the world. For example, ChatGPT can be used to gather information on a specific topic, summarize long articles, or provide explanations for complex concepts. This has the potential to revolutionize the way we approach learning and research, making it faster, more efficient, and more accessible.

Another way that ChatGPT is changing our understanding of the world is by breaking down language barriers. ChatGPT can generate responses in multiple languages, making it a valuable tool for communication between people who speak different languages. This can help to facilitate international communication and collaboration, bridging gaps between people from different cultures and backgrounds.

The impact of ChatGPT on human knowledge and understanding is a topic of growing importance, as more and more people begin to realize the potential of AI in transforming the way we interact with information and understand the world around us. At its core, ChatGPT represents a major shift in the way we think about language processing and machine intelligence. This has the potential to fundamentally change the way we gather, store, and analyze information, and it has already begun to make a significant impact on our ability to understand and utilize vast amounts of data.

One of the most notable ways in which ChatGPT is affecting human knowledge and understanding is through its ability to process large amounts of data in real-time. This has the potential to revolutionize the way we analyze data and make decisions based on that data. For example, ChatGPT can be used to quickly and accurately identify trends and patterns in large data sets, making it possible for businesses and organizations to make informed decisions in real-time. This has the potential to dramatically increase efficiency and accuracy in decision-making processes, and it is already being used to improve outcomes in industries such as finance and healthcare.

In addition, ChatGPT is also playing a key role in advancing the field of natural language processing. As more and more people use ChatGPT to interact with computers and machines, it is providing a rich source of data that can be used to further improve language models and machine intelligence. This, in turn, will further improve the ability of ChatGPT to understand and interpret human language, leading to even more advanced AI systems in the future.

Furthermore, the integration of ChatGPT into various educational platforms is also having a profound impact on human knowledge and understanding. For example, ChatGPT can be used to provide students with personalized learning experiences, allowing them to learn at their own pace and in a way that best suits their individual needs. This can greatly improve student engagement and overall outcomes, and it is helping to create a more inclusive and effective education system for all learners.

Despite these benefits, there are also limitations to ChatGPT's impact on human knowledge and understanding. One of the biggest challenges is ensuring that the information generated by ChatGPT is accurate, reliable, and trustworthy. This requires ongoing efforts to refine and improve the algorithms and models used by ChatGPT, as well as ensuring that the data fed into the system is high-quality and free from biases.

Another challenge is ensuring that the integration of ChatGPT into various systems and platforms is done in a way that is ethical and transparent. This requires careful consideration of the privacy and security implications of ChatGPT, as well as ensuring that the technology is used in a way that is fair and just to all users.

Overall, the impact of ChatGPT on human knowledge and understanding is a complex and multifaceted issue. While there are many benefits to this technology, it is important that we approach its integration into our lives and systems with caution and care, taking into consideration the potential limitations and ethical considerations. By doing so, we can ensure that ChatGPT becomes a powerful tool for improving our understanding of the world around us and making better-informed decisions.